PAPER LIPS.

LLEWELLYN GANNON MUNZING

To write *Paper Lips*, I revisited and re-edited 20 years worth of my poetry. These poems were preserved on whatever I could grab in a moment of inspiration, like napkins, receipts, junk mail and of course endless journals.

The poetry is organized to tell the story of my path through love, loss and transformation. It's part of my history and the journey of my heart. A coming of age and beyond. Besides a handful of poems, the majority were written when I was between the ages of 15 and 28 years old.

I used the concept of chemistry blended with the seasons to describe the 4 chapters. This is because many of the metaphors used in my poetry equate the human experience with the balance and power of natural elements. It is woven with abstract meanings and thoughts.

The photography is a dreamy take on the feelings and context behind the poems. While I was editing my poetry I became really inspired by the imagery going through my head. I wanted to express these new creative thoughts, so I decided to transfer some of them into photographs.

I created a series of self portraits, one a week for one full year. I selected the pictures that best represent the narration of this book. There are 35 that appear. The photos were captured with a Canon 5D S R accompanied by a Canon EF 28-300mm f/3.5-5.6L IS USM and a Canon EF 50mm f/1.4 lens. The photos were processed and manipulated in Adobe Photoshop, circa 2017.

TABLE OF CONTENTS

THE ALCHEMIST:

TABLE OF CONTENTS

TABLE OF CONTENTS

I dedicate this book to every person it took to help me see. An extra glance back at true love and a secret smile because it's mine f o r e v e r.

C   D   J   M   J   J   M

PROEM:

PAPER AIRPLANES

This isn't about letting you know
that I hear your voice.
That your words linger, crimson
wounding, poetic.
Making me stronger
much more empathetic.
This isn't about sending a message
into the ether.
Altering karma.
Believe what you'd like to
this isn't about you.

This is about all of the others.
Those who got lost
following what their heart knew.
Those who end up
in the places I've gone through.
It's a love letter
to the ones who broke like me.
Who then picked up the pieces.
To those who kept dreaming.
A dream that the puzzle fit.
Within me I found you..
It's the promise I made
all the things I would do...
It's a ticket for a trip
on a folded up airplane
destined to land where it's thrown.
With the words on the paper
I already threw.
We move on in our rhythm
create something new.
It doesn't matter if my drifting words
reach you.
The future looks different and special
without you.
Danced with a stranger
under a new moon.
Still can't forget you.
That dreams always come true.

THE SEEKER:

YEARN

Early
morning
thirst.
Moist
stems
snapping
in the
wind.
Water
drips to
earth.

Drops Of Me

SILENT
MOTHER

So beautiful she looked
so lost.
The queen of words unspoken.

Her majesty, who rules my heart
and all hearts
that are broken.

#1 DIARY ENTRY
AGE: 15

I remember the first time I realized the power a mind can have over another mind. By power I mean the ability to use thoughts and feelings to get what you want without having to say a word.

I think it was the summer after 7th grade, my grandma was in town visiting. She would fly in from Chicago once a year, rent us a car and we would drive to Seaside. There was always this artist posted up on the strip who signed his work with, Savage. He created beautiful chalk portraits and characters. There would be a crowd gathering, watching. We'd stop and watch but could never afford one. This year I had the $10.00 it cost to have the character drawn of me, but not the $20.00 it cost to have the portrait drawn. I secretly wanted the portrait more. A lot more.

When I sat down to have my character drawn, I looked at him in his eyes and I knew and I felt the simple truth, that I was worthy of a portrait. He looked back at me and said, "I must draw your portrait."

WILD FIRE

From the meadow
filled with wild flowers
under a conspiring sky
I see the border of a forest.
Dark, in nature
washed in captivating mystery.
Far in the distance
I hear water falling from a cliff
moved by the current
of gravity
on this part of its journey.
I feel the wind
pick me up.

NTRY

AGE: 15

Fuck you, Jake, full of lies! Full of yourself. How good you must feel, conquering your newly charted territory. You sounded so sweet as you lied to me. With no appreciation of what I was giving up. Trust. A scary word and feeling that I can't seam to grasp. And just like that, the shreds I was able to pull together, gone. Ripped apart. You were able to manipulate the truth so well that you believed yourself. So did everybody else. I don't hate you, my friend. I should have trusted the details, read between the lines. It's not your fault I feel this way, I brought it upon myself. When will I learn?

JOHNNY

Johnny comes to town riding his BMX getaway car.

Leading the rebellion as I ride upon the handlebar.

Apocalyptic teenage frowns.

We learned to fly, underground.

Lawless love and we got caught

by rumors of our reckless plot.

Johnny, what's got into you? Your eyes changed to a deeper blue.

Got a matching wing tattoo. A stinging, cryptic, I love you.

We'd push and shove, we held on tight.

We'd fight and love and love and fight.

He told me lies, my first torn heart.

...I cried tears that turned to art.

Johnny, meet me down the road. You always know just what to say.

Paging you our secret code, one hundred thousand times a day.

In and out of window panes.

Miles in the Portland rain.

Carved a heart in wet cement.

Somebody paved over it.

Johnny, don't you feel it, too? Our time is here, and nearly through.

I guess these feelings must be true. Someday I'll be over you.

The way I left, the words I said...

Whether he's alive or dead.

I took him back into my stride

but he lied, and he lied, and he lied, and he lied.

Johnny, did I hurt you, too? You're such a lovely shade of blue.

I press my lips to yours, there's only one thing left for me to do.

I earned these wings, away I flew.

I guess I really learned from you.

Whisked Away

F A I R Y T A L E

Her name is Sleeping Beauty, as the fairytale goes.
Born the queen of endless dreams, she hid amongst the shadows.
In the Land of Ever After, a wilder love still grows.
She ruled upon a windy throne, her scepter was the rose.

Her cupid's bow and arrow lips would bring him to his knees.
To wake her from a restless sleep and steal her from the breeze.
With big bright eyes that glistened, in a glance could lure and tease.
A pounding heart ablaze that longed for love to set it free.

Her hair was dark as raven, holding secrets of the night.
Yes, the knight in shining armor for her nobly did fight.
Then kissed her face so gently, turned and rode out of her sight.
As her raven hair flew in the freezing wind and cold moonlight.

The same old fairytale and as the fairytale goes.
She pricked her finger hard against a thorn upon the rose.
A never ending story through the ages will unfold.
She woke up, alone and dizzy. Cried her eyes out, oh what a pity.
Heard the mirror, mirror saying, she ain't pretty.
More lies that she'd been sold.

Had a change of heart. Life is better when you love yourself.
A change of plans. Never live for someone else.
Her first command was to leave behind the fables.
Her fairytale's untold.

Light In The Dark

SOULMATES

Someone's whispering.
Yeah, something's coming.
Someone wants to know
where you've been hiding.
Something turned your way
and now it's running.
Someone wants your love.
Yeah, something's coming.

Drifting into space
can be so blinding.
Came back took your place
among the dying.
And although our lives
have come and they've gone
I still know those eyes
though it's been so long.

I have never seen
your face before.
In the light of day
your shadow disappears.
I know those eyes
and they make me sore.
Reflecting the moonlight
on my tears.

WEST BOUND

It's him again
our west bound train.
In, off of platform C.
He's pressed against
the crowded wall
and doesn't notice me.
Enraptured at the sight of him
encompassed by his book.
Display my longing, helpless mind
upon my displaced look.
He's off, into the elevator
I sit in the train.
I ride away into the dark
he slides up to
the rain.

The Look

A FANTASY

Your eyes, the first thing I see
when I wake up in my fantasy.
When you kissed me goodbye
you said believe in your eyes.

Served the dream, served with loyalty.
Ruled the dream like royalty.
Dreamt the words that you would say.
Stole my beating heart away.

Hot and cold and steamy.
Your embrace could free me.
Fell deep in love with the ecstasy.
Starring you, in my fantasy.

A world that's painted by me.
A small piece of my fantasy.
And I could do this all night.
I could do this all my life.

Served the dream of unity.
Blurred lines between you and me.
Struck a deal with destiny.
Blurry lines of reality.

Come and reign. Don't walk away.
Crown you king if you choose to stay.
You can't forget the way that it feels
so come out and play.

A perfect crush, not some mistake.
This time we can stay awake.
I will teach you to believe.
Come away to my fantasy.

Touched the dreams of lucidity.
Drove the force inside of me.
Faced the charge of sorcery.
Jusl my vulnerability.

Served the dream with loyalty.
Ruled the dream now I'm royalty.
Flames rise fast in disarray.
Come and carry me away.

Free To Decide

TROUBLE

Stuck somewhere in the middle of
holding on and falling down.
Swept me off my feet so fast
I still can't feel the ground.

I'm trapped in my bubble
I don't know the danger yet.
I don't know the hidden trouble
how bad it can really get.

You came here for something.
You want it? I got it.
Possess me, mess with me.
It could get erotic.

I know you. You're Trouble.
Lust without a heart or soul.
No substance, no matter.
A charge, a heavy pull.

Your hand on my face.
A waste of such a thrilling ride
if you run away. If you're
scared you'll run and hide.

#3 DIARY ENTRY
AGE: 22

We're friends. I've had many friends. Some grow into beautiful lifelong journeys and some end with short lessons at hand. Some things I've learned from you are to respect my friend's time and ambitions. Not to stand in the way of their dreams. I love when my friends have a lot of dreams. That's what I admire about you.

I'm going to set some goals for myself.

1. With or without Collin's friendship, I'm moving to the mountain this winter 2002-2003

2. Take a creativity class at PCC. Photography, creative writing, sketching, poetry, painting, or all of the above. This year.

3. Follow my intuition. Always!

Where I Go

LOVE ME

Love me
or leave me alone.

Lift me up
in your arms
or let me down slow.

Love me
lead me home.

Or leave this place
without a trace.
If you have to go.

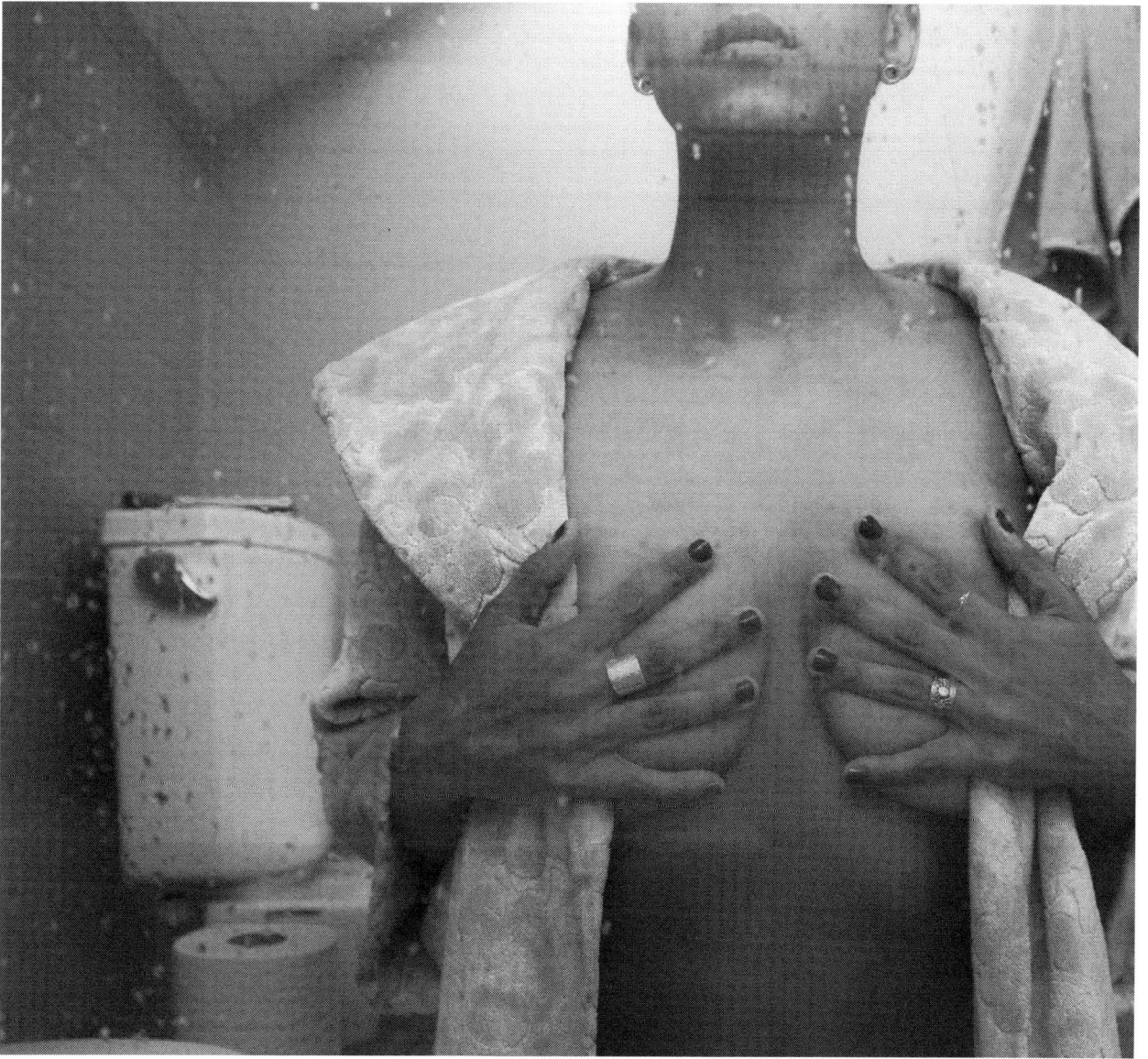

Covered Nude

WANT

I want you
so badly
it's hot
and it hurts.
I took off
my jacket
and took off
my shirt.
To ease up
the tension.
You cunningly
froze.
I started
sweating
ripped off all
my clothes.
The air's
thick and sultry.
Don't you
agree?
Now were
swaying
like the ocean
in the dark
and deep.
Nothing
in between us
but your
wicked games.
Can you handle
the heat?
Do we want it
the same?

THE BELOVED:

SUNLIGHT

Sunlight beating the
hemisphere, lighting the path
blinding my vision.

Splendor In The Grass

LOVE IS

You told the truth
and that's what matters.
Heavy hearts are built to shatter.

Based our love on trust and lust.
The beauty on the dents
and rust.

My Wishes

DREAM PARTY

Blow away the darkness run away hand in hand. My dream party is finally coming true. Now I'm drifting into...

MASTERPIECE

This is my masterpiece.
A watery love
rushing forth
the tide inside a pulsing vein.
This is my right.
This is my life.
My will
under dark stars
that are falling like the rain.
I have planned on this moment
for ages.
Lifetimes and beyond
moving heaven and earth
to be with you.
The current is much too strong
to swim to the shore.
I lay back
and float along
in love
and into the
dark blue.
Somewhere in your eyes
I am there
like a care.
Longing to be lost
but I'm there
staring back at me.
We went swimming in the stormy night.
Reflect each other's light.
Now we're drifting out to sea.

I find home
in my masterpiece.

Swept Away

WHAT IS YOURS AND MINE

I'll say the words that make you want to crawl out of your skin. I'll walk you through the steps it takes to learn to feel again. In this world the well runs deep. In the dark are wounds you keep. Afraid to sleep, afraid to dream to know I fell in love. In this world there isn't time to hide from fear, you're not fine. I always feel a little scared. Perhaps, for you are mine.

Twin Souls

AROUND AGAIN

You flew by, caught my eye. I knew we belonged together.
When it started to snow, I knew I'd wait forever.

You turned and came around. Our friendship turned into lust.
I'm yours, just don't let me down. You're mine, and I give my trust.

Our passion is so igniting. I call you my best friend.
You're bad, and so exciting. We make love never end.

You bring out the best in me. You set my sorrow free.
You bring up my deepest hurt and you make me feel so weak.

Then I woke up all alone. Dropped by, but you weren't at home.
No answers, no way to know. Couldn't be reached by phone...

I feel the season end. You lie to my face again.
You turn it around on me, I throw it right back and then-

You want to leave? Then do. Threaten me, I'll threaten you.
Blaming, renaming... Grieving. So much noise, I can't see through.

The squall clears and I'm here all alone, to pick up this mess.
With my pride on its throne, inside my crumbling chest.

Before, you come around again. Breaking me down again.
You're asking to be my friend. Promise to change, and then-

I start melting into you. What you need, I give in to.
Cause you feel like all of my wildest dreams coming true.

The most love we've ever been in, just hold my body tight.
Just kiss my skin again and let's never ever fight.

We're smooth, so strong together. Whisper my name forever.
I think you're beautiful, you think that I'm so clever.

Spending all of my spare time with the past on my scared mind.
It's colder, I'm fine. It's just pouring down rain outside.

But every time you stop talking, change of heart, you're walking
back out the door on me. You want a fight... And then leave.

I bring out the worst in you, you're breaking my heart again.
What you're saying can't be true. But you say it, and then-

The storm's rolling in again. Lightning strikes, we come up dead.
Frozen in winter, now it's snowing inside my head.

Will you come around again and poison my cup again?
Or laugh off the past, crawl back into my veins and then-

Set me on fire. For a moment- We burn in desire.
Will you love me forever? My sweet little liar.

JUST SMILE

I just smile
my useless smile.
Hold my breath
and try to sustain.
Let him leave
it's just for a while.
When he turns to go
my smile remains.

He just smiles
a lifeless smile.
Feels like death.
Inside of me grieves.
Give it space.
Cause that's just my style.
After he goes
I fall to my knees.

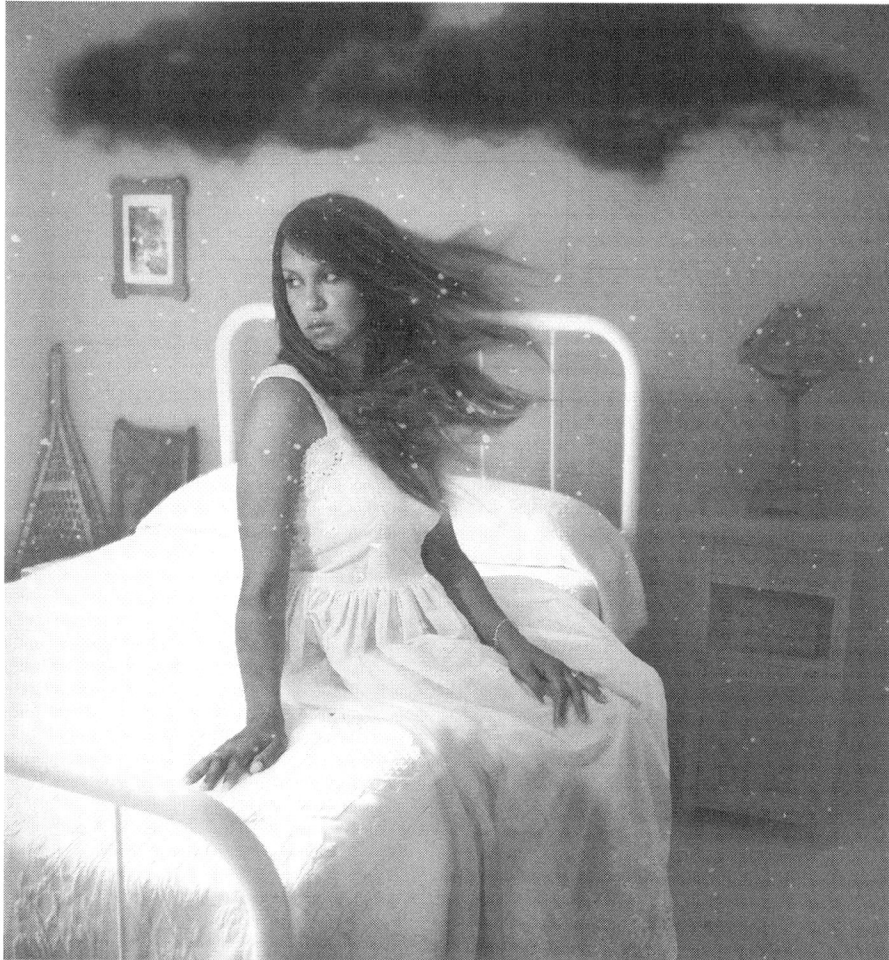

Our Bedroom

FORECAST

Hello, my stormy weather friend.

Are your skies turning black? Do you need me again?

C R U E L

The coldest night's upon us and the wind can be cruel.
The daylight slipped away, now we're stuck out here like fools.

Battling the blindness as the tears whip off my face.
Better hold you tighter to be sure we keep our place.

The biting wind is merciless, even on our knees.
Will not let us catch our breath and will not hear our pleas.

If we stood upon the sun we'd want the wind this cool.
Here amongst the icicles the bitter wind is cruel.

A FIGHT

Don't give up, without a fight.

I can't see on this moonless night.

I'm too afraid to speak, besides

I know in my heart, it's not right.

I'm gone, I'm wrong, but don't lose sight.

There's no one else, please hold on tight.

Although I swing at ghosts, in spite

and I may scream and I may bite.

I love you after all, despite...

So please don't leave

without a fight.

Escape Back

BLAME

Come and kiss the fault away.
Come warm my heart; cry my name.
Or spend a lifetime, come what may
sleeping with your mistress, Blame.

RISK NIGHT

Risk another night.
Risk another whisper.
Believe.
The sun is just a star
in the blue.

Risk all of your life.
Race into the future
with me.
I've already run away
with you.

Please don't tell me
the end is near.
Now I need you here.
Together with the stars as our sight.

When we're gone away
the stars will remember these days.
How we made it through
the darkest night.

US

We really are different

I walk on the sunshine that feeds inspiration and brightens my days.

You bow to the moonlight

you worship the dark night, and when the sun rises you hide from the rays.

Kiss The Moon

SINGING ALONE

We wandered, I sang. You clumsily humming.
Remaining the same, but change was coming.

You dropped your pitch, your melody ceases.
My rhythm stands still, the volume increases.

Two different beats to the tune of our song.
Together and lost somehow never seemed wrong.

I looked back and noticed you singing along
sliding along
tension was gone.
You sounded and looked so good, all on your own.
Moving along
singing alone.

KISSES IN THE WIND

You're like the breath of an icy cold winter
that blows through
freezing the day.

That blows out the lights while it blows me a kiss.
Then it's just
blowing away.

#4 DIARY ENTRY
AGE: 23

I'm still so mad and hurt! Why did I fall in love with him? From the very beginning it has been so hard. I could never fully reach him and didn't feel very important when I was with him. I thought I enjoyed the challenge. The closer we became the more special I felt. The more I get to know him the more I realize that he has no control over his emotions.

SOME DON'T

Some don't grow. Stand back and watch, but still don't grow.
And even worse, don't want to know.
I guess that's the way it goes, we're just crazy and it shows.

Will they change? Will you ever see them change?
You give them all you've got and they still settle for the rot
bathing in suffer that remains. Still no change.
Some won't grow.

OUR FIRE

We get together
no choice or right.
We're flame to flame
when we're heart to heart.
Passion is flammable
and so is our trigger.
You're the only one
who understands.
Our fire grows bigger.
It fills the room
eats all the oxygen.
Engulfs all we've become.
It's what we've been living for.
With devouring strength
fire consumes.
Fire has to feed.
Until the only things left standing
is me here in disbelief
and everything
I feel tonight.

Lit Up The Night

H O M E

This house feels like a home.
At the same time, it's time to go.
The walls are drenched in satire.
Where there's smoke
there's always fire.

This house held everything.
My life, my love, and my dreams.
My fear that won't let me go
in this place
that we call home.

This roof was here for me
through the rain that set me free.
Gave me room to grow my dreams.
In this house
I became me.

These walls are burning down.
In the glow the truth is found.
Soon there will be no home to go home to.
Just stories of a place
that only we knew.

WITHOUT YOU

I'm fading and I can't steer.
I guess I'm fading out of here.
I'm fading to without you.

I'm sorry, I turned to you.
I looked to you. I looked through you
and saw myself without you.

I'm missing, it's nothing new.
I have found myself often times
just floating to without you.

It's in my head. I'm alright.
Just leave me here so I can
find myself without you.

I came here cause you were stuck
free around you.
I came here to give you love
me around you.
I came here, I'll pay the cost
bleeding down you.
I came here to give you up
leave without you.

IN MY OPINION

She sees me like I see me, and we think I'm crazy.

Me, My Mask And I

LAST TIME

The last time I had to choose, I lost my way and ended up here.
Kissed a myth in the pouring rain
pretending it was you.

The last time I'll play your game, fall for your pity, kiss your shame.
I believe you will never change
and you believe it, too.

OBJECTIFIED

You and I and the wake of forever.
You and I thought you live for forever.
You and I fell in love and the earth quaked.
Changed directions and we're well on our way.

You and me and the wake of forever.
You and me in the heat of the desert.
You and me in the thunder and lightning.
That was then, now it's you and me dying.

A Glimpse

THE MOMENT

So this is pain.

This is a lifetime worth of change.

Let go today.

My same old heart, just rearranged.

So this is freedom.

The ceaseless thunder shakes your core

echoing leaving.

Sounds like me, walking out the door.

THE LABYRINTH:

RIPE

Fruit is falling fast
all around me. Ripe, dying.
Plenty astounding.

MY
WEAKNESS

F a r e w e l l
c o n f e s s i o n s
I hope you felt
the same.
If I misjudged you
blame it on
my aim.

Ocean Meets Sky. Goodbye

A L O N E

Alone. You have stolen the sun from the sky. I suppose you couldn't leave, alone.

YOU

You are overgrown
unmanageable, unruly.
From the outside
a forest wall.
From the inside
you are lost.
Depleted of sunlight.
That which hasn't made it out
dwells forever in the depths
of the shadows that weave through the vines
that have grown together.
Twisting, choking
continuously following in circles
and strangling the life out of itself
for the very purpose
of dying.

LONG GOODBYE

I know you had to go.
I tried to set you free.
I thought I could afford
the cost in pain.
This time we sealed the deal.
Goodbye, and you kissed me.
Then stepped aboard an empty
late night train.

I have torn apart my soul
in the name of finding you.
All I've ever found
was one last try.
I know we'll meet again
and our love will be as true.
Next time it's time for us
to say goodbye.

AT BEST

At best, they tell me
without you here.
At best I find myself
drowning in my fear.
At best I miss you.
At worst I die.
At best, I told you
while looking in your eyes.
At best when dreaming
or lying to my friends.
At best we're both lost
but we'll meet again.
At best, couldn't feel more wrong.
Am I a fool for holding on?
The fool who can't let go
who may never know
at best, you're gone?

SAFE FROM HOME

You must feel safe cause I don't know
where you sleep at night.
Safely tucked in sweet illusion
pretending you were right.

You're mistake'less in forsake'ness.
Only in your dreams.
With a new twist... My replacement.
No time to cry for me.

You may be safe from my hands.
Slipped away into the night.
Safe in the fact that darkness
steals time and steals your sight.

Don't you see it crawling towards you?
Creeping up, in your mind?
Lonely, nowhere to turn to
in the corner of your eye.

Can't you hear me like a heartbeat
pound on these walls, alone?
Can't you feel me, like a heartbreak?
Or are you safe from home?

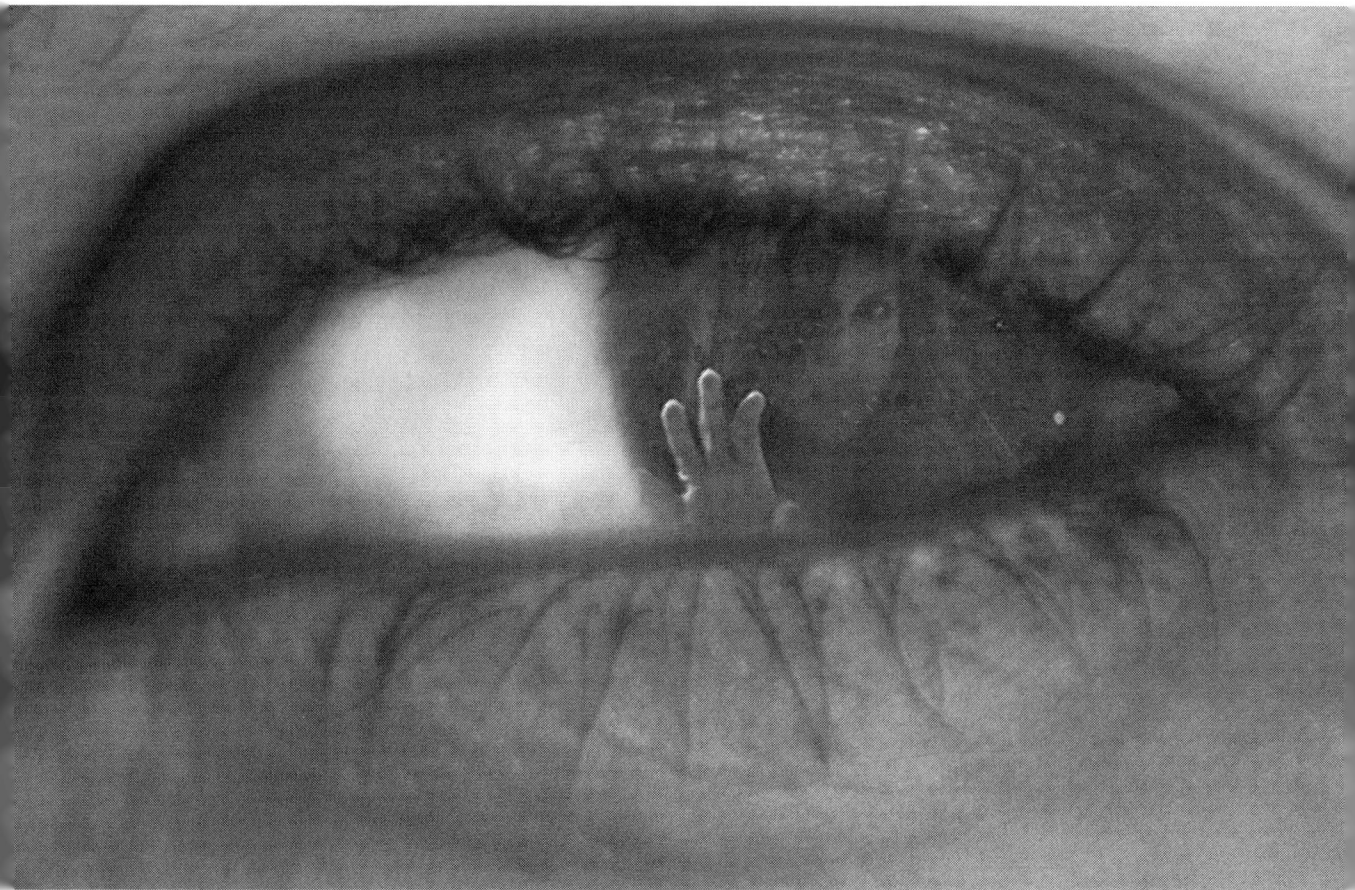

In My Eyes

GRAB YOU

It's cold to the touch.
I wish I still had you.
I want you so much
sometimes I could just grab you
and steal you away from her.
I swear I love you more.
Trapped out in the old
no key to unlock the door.

KNOWING YOU

Knowing you
the way I did.
Through your eyes
under your skin.
That part of me
you haven't left.
Caught inside me
in a trap.
I know too much
but you know that.

#5 DIARY ENTRY
AGE: 25

I really need to tell you that I'm sorry. I'm sorry that I left you. Looking back it wasn't worth it. I chose the wrong path. I know you're beyond caring by now. We both know we couldn't have made it work. But you were my best friend. I wish I would have stayed and treated you better. Hard times were coming for me and I was trying to out run them. I went back to him. I walked into my own trap of betrayal and loss. You're alright, but I'm not. You will always be my inspiration. I have loved you since I was 15 and I always will. I'm sorry.

Feels Like Roses

YOUR LIPS

Heard your secret in a soft sigh, lips betray you while you sleep.
Held your body through the last time that you ever felt at peace.
Giving up just comes so easy, when the truth is left denied.
Letting go is not as easy. I'd still kiss your lips that lied.

Stood beside you like a brother. Left you all alone to freeze.
Did I blow away your cover in the schoolyard, on my knees?
Waited- for what felt like lifetimes. Shared the dreams you tried to hide.
Lost my own way in the meantime. I'd still kiss your lips that lied.

All we built drowned in the last storm. I, the tempest. You, the sea.
When I shipwrecked on the rough shore, you were gone and I was free
to wonder all my life about you. A million tears I've cried.
If a single word were true, I'd still kiss your lips that lied.

The bluest eyes were yours in summer. You are looking through me.
I hear you're dreaming of some other... I'm still following the breeze.
Do you blame me, long lost lover? For the rain that never dried?
You can blame me for the thunder. I'd still kiss your lips that lied.

You blame me, we blame each other. Your soft lips that lied.
Say you'll never love another. Your wicked lips that lied.
With the fragile truth discovered, I'd still kiss your lips that lied.

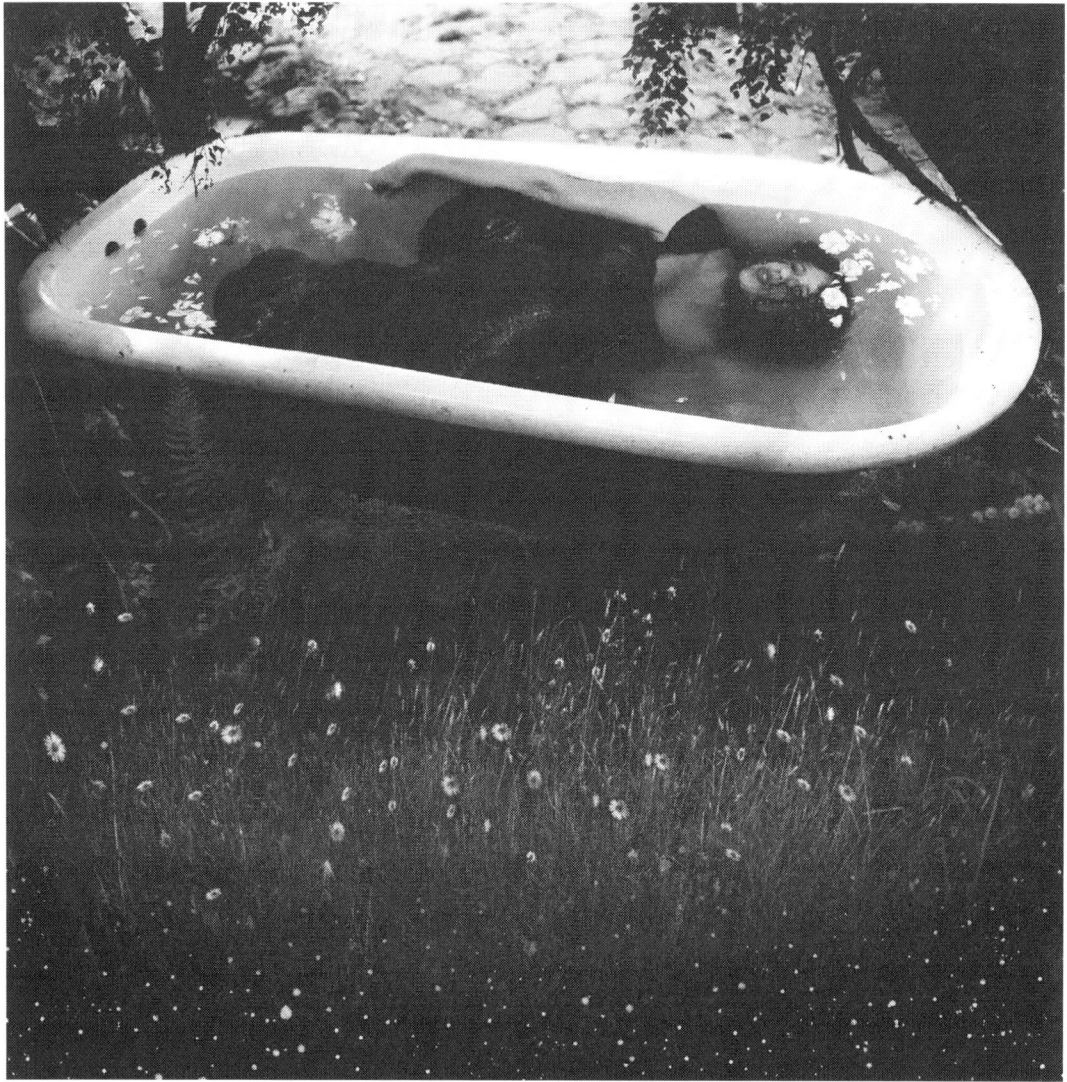

Apnea

RUNNING
AWAY

Our smoke
and dreams.
The only thing I can see.
I'm really not afraid
when you're holding me.
But he does.
You had to run.
Closing the one
opening you.

I can't move.
You're racing to the moon.
I wanna run away with you.
Because
you had to run.
Closing the one.
Opening you.

Running away
falling away
losing your way
dying away
flying away...

#6 DIARY ENTRY
AGE: 26

I know I promised I would never forget you. Now that I've been living without you for so long, I have kept my promise. Too much. I dreamt about you last night. It was the same nightmare I've had many times before. I'm at a party with our close friends. Everyone around me knows where and how you are. They are talking about you casually with minor details. I don't dare ask the questions I have about you. Even in my dream I understand that if you wanted me to know then you would have told me. So I stood there, pretending not to care. Acting like I'm not listening but the deepest feelings of loss and desperation crept in. I wanted more than anything to reach through someone and touch you. Instead I stood there smiling. Even in my dream.

CARRY ON

It isn't losing you that's giving me nightmares
I lay my troubled head upon.

I turned around so fast I missed you completely.
Turned back around and you were gone.

I know they tell me that silence is golden.
I'd give all my riches for your thoughts.

Echoing memories that are softly fading
are the only luxuries I've got.

I know the night is long, and haunting is its lonely song.
It isn't losing you that's giving me nightmares
that carry on.

C O N T R O L L E R S

We were born the controllers and we stand over you.
We're alluring and spiteful in all we say and do.
We can play with your dreams as we watch from a distance.
We can alter your faith with a breath of resistance.
When we're gone, you notice. Cause you crave our destruction
in your sad little world with your sad reproduction.
Yes, we know you, your habits, your addictions, desires.
We control you by feeding, or starving your fire.
The connections electric. The strongest that you'll find.
And that's the reason you suffer, we stay on your mind.
We captivate, complicate, we'll never let you go.
We love your taste, your warm embrace on our skin so cold.
There's a reason we call at night. A reason for you.
We don't tire of you, desire you... We get nightmares, too.
We're your first love, your last love. The one who broke your heart.
We're the grim reaper, soul keeper. You're the lovesick part.
And we're dancing on the grave. We're feeding on your clues.
Loss and lust makes us hungry and we're hungry for you.
Pray for freedom, redemption. You can break down and cry.
You want solace? Then don't ever look us in the eyes.
When you wake up, heart pounding, sweat rolling down your face.
You'll know we've been there, don't fear. We always leave a trace.
We can cure the emptiness that poisons your bloodstream.
We're closing in, come follow us back inside our dream.
You captivate, complicate. You never let me go.
Kiss my face, resume your place. These dreams are real, I know.
I don't care why. All my life, I'm all yours all night long.
Cause I, can't let you go. And I, can't believe you're gone.
You were born the controller and you've locked me in chains.
Shackled so tightly around me they're cutting my veins.
Goodbye, so long to you. Best in all the things you do.
Remember what goes around is coming right back at you...
And just like me in the twilight, before the night is through
you never feel alone, ache for home or long for someone new.

The Ghost In The Garden

10,000 DAWNS

Time passes by, I start to cry.
Slowly my grip's lost, solidity dies.
10,000 dawns, our love is gone.
I keep forgetting that I'm moving on.

THE CITY

Where I'm from
there's no room for reality
time for finality
and we go all the way around.
We wait forever
miss together
and when we cry
don't make a sound.

LIFE

All this time spent forging forgiveness.
Too proud to relive this
and too proud to say goodbye.
Do you feel like sorry's beyond you?
When you think of me
do you ever break down and cry?

In this life I'm dying to tell you
I can forgive you.
If you'd only let me try.
But you're running
so we're running out of time
to make amends in this life
for this lie.

Your silence... And no way to tell you.
No way to touch you.
Just my dreams in the night.
I've done time. I will never be your wife.
And I'm sorry
cause you bring out a part of me
I will never meet again
in this life.

What I Don't Know

GOOD AND GONE

If good means good
and bad means bad
then you're so good
and I'm still sad.

If bad means good
then you're so bad.
If good is gone
then you're the best
I've ever had.

PHANTOM

Phantom lover, it's not over. Haunt me, come and take today. Trap me in your twister with you blowing back to yesterday. Fall in love to your embrace. Rapture in your ghostly grace. Dreaming of a time that's gone by. New attraction, smooth chaos. Spinning in a twister with me weighing me with sudden loss. Stealing all my strength and breathe. Leave behind the smell of death. You're everyone, you're everything that's gone. Now I can't breathe. You never ending, haunting lovely revenant, I grieve. Phantom, dreams and I, makes three turning knives inside of me. Holding on to old dreams we had like you'll never say goodbye. Where all I've built and all I want revolves around your eyes. I know you from a past life. When you go there's just two knives. Phantom breaths, your days are over. Lost forever. Let me be. Or I may never love another. Vanished lover, set me free. You'll be back, I'll let you in. I'll fall... You'll break my heart again.

UPON PAPER LIPS

You became a distant life
sailed away into the night.
Cast aside
when I needed you the most.
You became the trail of a falling star.
Light lost
but that's who you are.
Then in my darkest hour
you are the ghost.
I can go on forever
crying over what was never.
Just two lost hearts
aboard two separate ships.
I know there is no way back
but I always feel better
when I'm kissing your paper lips.
If you ever pass my way
looking for the words I may never say
pounding out of
my calloused fingertips.
Take these black stains of regret
words never spoken
dripping wet.
Pouring out
upon paper lips.

Drenched Petals

THE CASTLE

Here behind these walls I am safe in control.
Here where the atmosphere is predictable.
This luxurious castle where I spend my days.
Nothing can burn me, I'm blocked from all rays.

Here, locked up in the safety I can't feel too much.
Escaped to a place walls too thick to feel touch.
I promise to never come down from my tower.
The last time I landed I lost all my power.

She is safe in a locket, the girl with the wings.
Who thought she knew you, thought she knew everything.
Staring into the sun as you wandered away.
Make-believing that you would return here someday.

The scars on my heart are the map to moving on.
Can't wonder if my love is missed when it's gone.
Your mystery was fading, you had to be going.
There's something so haunting about never knowing.

I built here a castle out of ruins, to survive.
And I'm just glad that I made it through alive.
That falling was finding my dreams can be lessons.
Believe, when I tell you these walls are a blessing.

Falling Angel

QUESTION?

What are you going to do?
Love him until you die?
Waiting until you meet again
is how you'll spend your time?
What are you going to say?
You've been counting up the hours?
You've been waiting for this moment
gave his memory all your power?

ONE

Ready or not,

                it's reckoning day.

I'm not ready for this,

                      I'm too afraid.

I said

        ready or not,

                there's no where to run.

You can't hide from yourself,

                    we are all one.

SMILE

Life, glancing her way
reflecting black.
She, frowning at life
then life frowning back.
Couldn't feel sunshine.
Her heroes have died.
Hiding in dark eyes
was lonely inside.
There was distant light
rippling through water
of the damp morning.
Saw Midnight's daughter.
Felt nothing. It was
better than before.
The sky, beautiful.
She stared a bit more.
Then felt rays of hope.
The dark held her fears
and offered goodbyes
soaked in Midnight's tears.
Up came the sun
from out of the black.
She, smiling at life.
Her life smiling back.

A SONG

Always romantic
almost nothing cuts deeper.
I gently rest my head upon the speaker.
Feel the connection
the frequencies hopping.
I let it rock me.
Structure, dirty talking.
The hallways echoing
wattage and amp'age.
It's time to let this affair do its damage.
There's a song I love
to sing really loud.
Drowned out the thoughts
in my front lobe crowd.
Hide away in a melody cloud.
Hit repeat and ride it round and around.
I screamed that song
so fucking loud.
There are stranger things
music is power.
Never loved so hard
inside of an hour.
I'm not alone, the stereo's on.
I found myself within
a song.

#7 DIARY ENTRY
AGE: 27

On my own, on too many sleepless nights, my anxiety is reduced to a numb memory. Here in the numbness a new realization has been born. You are not gone at all and I don't miss you. You're still as real as ever in my life and though you are not standing in front of me, we will never be apart. We will never be no more. It's the past that is as certain as the present. It can't be taken away. So it's mine forever. And we don't need a future to live happily ever after in the past. I know it is for me to decide what that looks like and feels like, on too many sleepless nights.

THE ALCHEMIST:

BREADTH OF VIEW

Crisp, cool air. Whispers
blowing past what has
split away.
Glistening and gray.

FOREVER

I felt my heart break. Now it's stronger than ever. I had to say g o o d b y e so don't ever say never. There is one thing I have that this life cannot sever. I will love again but I will love you f o r e v e r.

Return Home

DARK AND DANGEROUS

Some souls have never felt
the dangerous dark.
May never breathe as deeply
as I did
the moment I left day.
Don't know the battle
of the journey
into self.
Or bare the scars of love
scars of loss
from someone else.
Some don't wake up at night.
Dream of daylight safety bliss.
Always reflecting perfect light.
Some souls make it through
unscathed.
Unmoved.
Unlike my soul.
I bare the markings
from the overgrown trail.
You want to peek into the unknown?
Leave the safety of your precious mind?
Life must be getting dull.
Still afraid of the shadows
the uncharted terrain.
We all chase the sunlight
but the day always turns to night.
You are always close to home.
I followed my heart
into the dark and dangerous.
And I got what I came for.
So much bigger, so much more.
I found truth.

SCARS

We are connected by scars
connected to the past.
I'll feel this way again.
As I pass by, kiss me fast.

We are bound by this feeling
we embodied to feel.
We give to each other
that what soulmates reveal.

FROM MY SOUL

I mopped up the sorrow that spilled from my soul and into my veins like a sickness, a madness. Changed my expression and changed all of my goals. Spilled out of my eyes to a puddle of sadness.

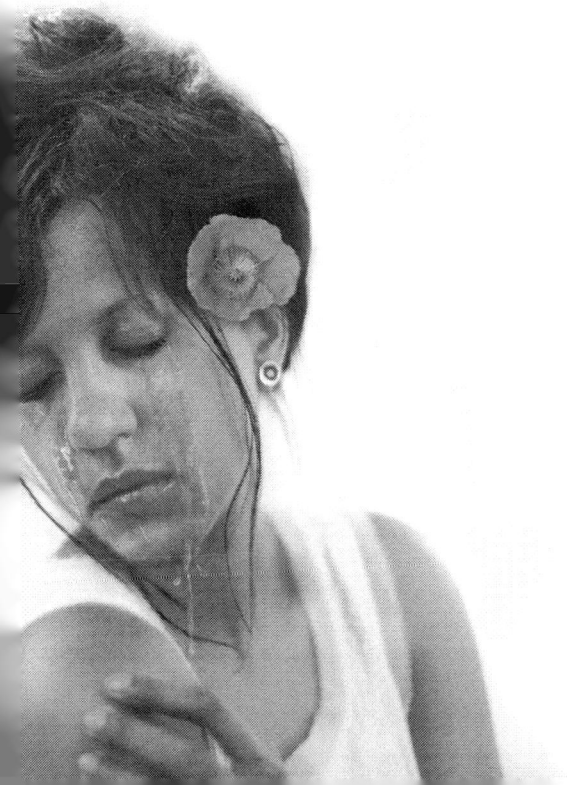

I Have Cried For You

MYSELF

Falling
in
love
with
myself
on
a
world
in
my
hands
while
sunlight
streaks
down
my
face
like
tears.

Love And All

GET IN LINE Take your place at the end of the line and wait for your turn to move up. You can either be patient, wait to get noticed, or you can attempt to cut. If you decide to be patient, it may take a lifetime to reach the front of the line. If you decide to cut, be charming and swift, for the end of the line is the fine.

RETROGRADE

The world is moving retrograde
history is calling.
There's something seeping into me
I can feel it crawling.
The world is moving retrograde
my luck is changing.
There's something flowing out of me
the world's obtaining.
The world is moving retrograde
makes me fall much faster.
Eclipse the precious past
shine on ever after.

THE DEFENDANT

I was a mess; I could love you more today.
Even though I packed my bags
and I turned and walked away.
I was too young, too sick to love you right.
Too blind to deal with the night.
Too hollow to give anything.
That's why you never wore my ring.
A liar never means to make you cry...
That's why I left without saying goodbye.

YOURS

There's nothing you can do
I don't hate you.
No place you can hide
I can't see through.
Nothing left to say
I believe you.
When you ran away
you took me too.

ONLY HERE TONIGHT

I'll let you feel my strength tonight
I'll let you see my light.
I'll let you see me at my best
but only here tonight.
I'll lay what happened on the floor
gracefully in spite.
I'll speak to you forgotten words
but only here tonight.

The Dreamers Gown

OLD LOVE

Dear devotion
trapped inside my heart
without one teardrop wasted.
Thank you for the love, loss
and confusion I have tasted.
If not for you I couldn't be
am not
and never would.
Not even in a million years.
I'd never know I could.
So, thank you for my bleeding heart
that hasn't let me sleep.
And flaw-full love affairs
in which
the benefits I reap.

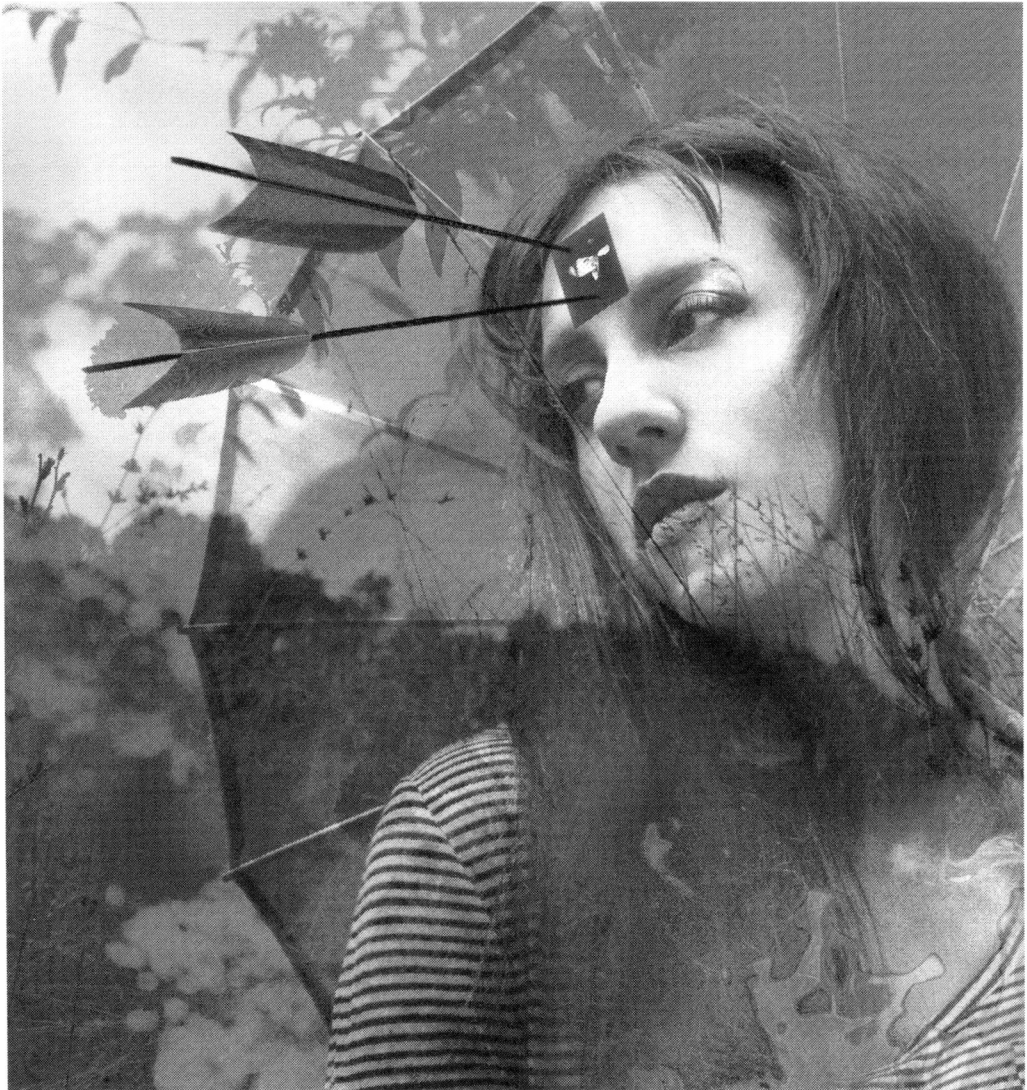

He and I

IN STARLIGHT

At times I'd like to know where you go
I want to see what you do.
Or just don't care, so much has happened
since I called us 'me and you.'
I finally get that we're just different
could have never made it last.
In my life your just a muse
that I'm in love with, from the past.
It seems I can live without you.
In the flesh, just not in thought.
I can truly say I'm happy.
That's more than you and I've got.
But still, sometimes by dream and starlight
you whisper you would stay.
We're in each other's arms, at last.
Then-   starlight fades away.

#8 DIARY ENTRY
AGE: 28

I don't mind living alone. If I'm not happy, if I'm not treated with love and respect then I will be alone. I'm not afraid to break off and walk away, if it's what I have to do to stop hurting this way. I know to cut it off at the source of the pain. I'm really feeling like I deserve more, I will find someone on the same page as me. I want a family. I want to be the lady of the house. The mother adored. Anyone can see that I've been drawn to certain people who are clearly not ready to be serious and honest. Less than trustworthy. Is it me who's not ready? I projected fear and it came alive. It devoured our safety and peace of mind. I don't want to be just getting by. If I end up with nobody, then that's just how it has to be. Then I will be alone and free. If I keep searching I'll find the best in time. When I'm alone I have my dreams of love by my side.

DOUBT

I could have been the girl
in the pictures by the sea.
I would have married you
if I didn't leave.
The one in your arms at sunset.
Soft vows that you believed.
I would wear your ring
and you would be deceived.

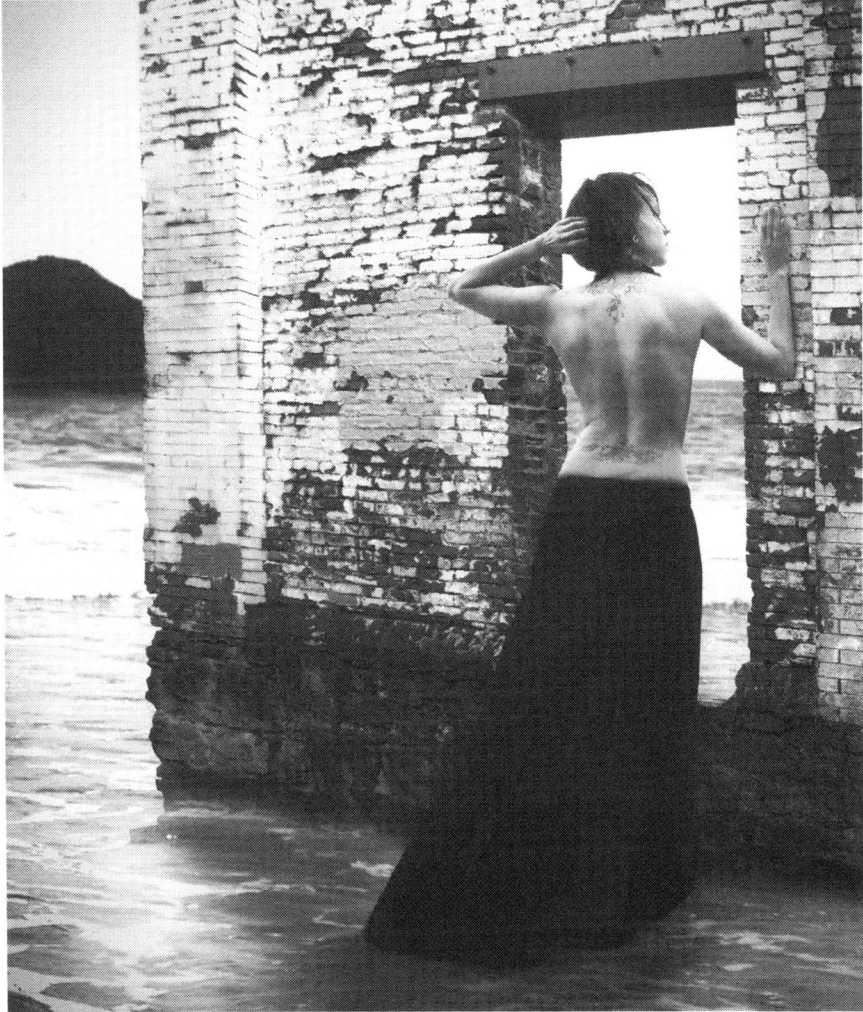

By The Sea

#9 DIARY ENTRY
AGE: 17

One of the greatest things in the world is to be yourself. No matter who you are, you were born with something unique that you and you alone posses. Embrace it. You have to enjoy it and explore it.

THE OBJECT OF MY AFFECTION

There is a new reason
I wake in the morning.
As an old drug
runs through my veins.
When I see those eyes
I forget I'm within me.
Nothing before them remains.
Is love unrequited
even a love at all?
An enemy, longing or friend?
It only took a second
to lose my grip and fall.
With nothing to show
but the wind.

BIRDCAGE

I opened the cage door and out flew the reasons that captured and bound me, for so long, to you. I'm not even looking and don't want to find the reasons I loved you, that out the cage flew.

RAINBOW

Let her fly.

Let her be one with

the sky. Let her be free.

The way we're all meant to be.

Let her die. Let her let go. Say goodbye.

You came to love, you came to cry

to see her live, to close her eyes.

To hold the hand of time she left behind.

Become the rainbow, the colors

that soar across the sky.

Let her become light

take flight. Let go and

let her fly.

THE LESSON

I still feel like it's turning
and will never settle down.
Round and round this vicious cycle
faster, faster, round and round.
It's my lesson left there burning
and it's all I've ever earned.
So I'll sink it in the river
like a lesson lived and learned.

MY FAVORITE

She's an old pair of blue jeans, worn in just right.
Frayed at the edges, stoned and ripped from the fight.
She takes to the streets with an armor of grace.
She has more style now than she did in those days.

I found her there, stashed at a second hand store.
Some fool walked away, left her at the door.
I brought her home, I consider myself blessed.
And to this day she always fits me the best.

The more time that passes, the better it gets.

My baby And Me

PASSING BY

I am alive today.
I am alive and all right.
With a newborn child
in a newborn life.

A moment is fleeting
and that moment is now gone.
They keep passing by
like the words to my song.

Try to hold a moment
like a lover you outgrew.
You'll leave as many
as many will leave you.

So, what else can you do?
I know one thing that's true.
Become one with the old
move on to the new.

THE RED ROSEBUD AND THE NIGHTINGALE

It was a love that was never intended
between the white rosebud and the nightingale.

A star-crossed story, true love unamended.
A typical romance, sort of fairytale.

In the barren valley of wind, thorns and twine
lived a white rosebud with petals of silk.

On the top of a mountain, perched on a vine
stood a bird who sang finer than all his ilk.

When the nightingale sang, the winter would thaw
in the lonely valley where the wild wind blows.

One night he was flying he looked down and saw
the most divine flower, the rarest white rose.

He flew down to sing to the delicate sight.
He could never forget the rosebud's perfume.

The rose thought, this kind of love couldn't be right.
She yearned for the night song, still wouldn't bloom.

She didn't yet know how to let this love in.
To bloom for the night, to bloom under moonlight.

The nightingale bravely flew into the wind.
The wind always prevails when faced with the night.

He gave her his song, unafraid of goodbye.
Beyond dulcet echos, their folklore lay dead.

She longs for his song, she's growing towards the sky.
Against the harsh sunset, her petals look red.

In The Garden

DRIVING FAST

I was at the wheel, still
searching for a place to go.
I changed the station
you were on the radio.
A melody transcending
felt a lot like kissing.
Everything is changing
is all I have to show.

Now I'm driving faster
then I ever drove.
Up the mountain
through the snow.
The sound of ever after
those haunting notes.
But it's where I learned
every word I wrote.

Now I'm riding faster
since you had to go.
Lost the signal
to the radio.
I never got an answer
just a rose.
Now I litter thorns
on the road I chose.

I'm Finally Flying

THE WILLOW

You can plunge

your roots deeper

than anything

I'll ever feel.

Give life to limb.

Then sever it

in void of deal.

I'll never try

to deny

it was real.

You can cut down

the willow.

Her soul

you can't steal.

G O L D

It's lonely chasing. Kissed the boys and made them cry.
My time was wasting, until I looked in your eyes.
I know that face. I needed someone to believe.
Unsure of space. I needed somewhere new to flee.

They're on the dance floor. We're still back at the tables.
Your eyes upon me, my eyes upon the 8.
Slipping out the side door, crying out you want more.
Never made it past my car, some things just can't wait.

In a different life, someplace. Love can't be erased.
Frozen in time and mine, untouchable, so cold.
I may never know if you know you touched my soul.
You put your hands on me and turned me into gold.

How can this be me? I can bleed without dying.
I couldn't see past the tears. They're finally drying.
All those beliefs are outdated old lies they told.
Now I believe that we're all turning into gold.

How can this be real? I can sing like a siren.
Now I can feel. Cut me free, at last I'm flying.
All of my fears overstated and growing old.
And worth its weight in words, I traded it for gold.

Paper Flowers

Thank you, Mike, for your love and friendship. And for our radiant story that carries on.

Printed in Great Britain
by Amazon